I0190778

1

Copyright © 2006 John Siwicki. All rights reserved.
No part of this publication may be reproduced,
stored in a retrieval system, or transmitted,
in any form or by any means, electronic,
mechanical, photocopying, recording, or otherwise,
without written permission of the author.

ISBN13978-09774118-4-9

For Library of Congress Cataloging-in-Publication Data
please contact publisher

Poetic Art Published by:

SLABYPRESS
W25952 State Road 95
Arcadia, WI 54612
U.S.A.

www.slabypress.com

Technical, Cover, and Book design by JBS

For information contact:
support@slabypress.com

INFLEXATION

POETRY OF LIFE

by John Siwicki

www.slabypress.com

Poems

Poems

The Time

The Time has come
For you to go with me
Sailing in the sky
Floating on the air
To another place
Where there is no time

I can't tell you what it's like
In a language
You would understand
In this place
Music is the Language
Of the land

The time has come for you
To go with me
Off to the land without time
Close your eyes
Step out of time

Song

Rice in the bowl
Strawberries on the spoon

In the background
The piano plays
A romantic tune

Voices of people
Laughter all around
Raise your glass
And time will sound

Silver, wood, and crystal glow
Our reflections grow

Myself I see
Face, and eyes
My heart is free!

Change the song?
Time to stop?
No, please don't!

I want it to play!
Just rest, hold the moment
In my memory forever
The watercolor of life

A raindrop in the ocean
The only one shining
Like the bright summer sun

Special time
Child's fun forever
The piano plays the tune

This time this song again
I will never see
Except in the reflection
Of my memory

Desire

While people meet
They really never know
The thoughts of the other's soul

They speak, listen, laugh
And they cry
But never share their real desire

But the future, it burns bright
And our dreams feed the fire

For our dreams are
A part of our soul
And the thoughts that
We never share

Suffer the soul
Lose the dream
Thoughts, love, and desire

Oh, but the future comes
Call it hope

The part of the soul
We call the fire

It does not rest
Even for a while

For time is a dream
Time is a thought

Our soul is a gift
And cannot be bought

But time is
An endless desire!

The Hour

The litany of which I speak
May ring to your ear
But to speak
Does not mean to hear
For time rings on the hour
A notion passed on by fear

We wait for time
To give us power
No choice of time or place
The signal like the hand we see
Familiar as the face

And the sound?
It falls from the tree
To catch it, gives us power
And to hold it, we think free
To hear it, the hour
And then it is time to be!

The Ocean & The Sky

We're part of the ocean
 Part of the sky
I thought part of a joke
And part of a lie
Until I saw with my own eye

I see it on your face
When you laugh and cry
Stars in the sky
Are up so high
Like dreams that fly

Light from the water I can't see
Light from the sky
Looks blue to me

A tear on your cheek
You don't have to speak
When life begins and ends

When we win and lose
The time we decide
Which path to choose

A smile comes after the storm
To laugh makes me feel warm
When a child is born
A blast from a trumpet's horn

A gift to share
A life that's unfair
Sometimes I laugh
Sometimes I cry

We're part of the ocean
Part of the sky
I thought part of a joke
And part of a lie
Until I saw with my own eye

Vacation

I woke to the sounds of the waves
Crashing into the beach
Hoping to see a whale
Greeting the Sun
But this was not the day

But what a day !
The sun shone from dawn to dusk
Coloring my skin rust

And then the morning to leave
I saw the sun lift from the sea
Leaving a wake of light behind

Oh, what a wonderful place
God made for you and me
And the gift of a memory by the sea
No one could give such a gift but He

Dreamer

Born long ago in a far away land
I sailed across the sea
To find a new home
My journey long, the sea rough
I had many dreams
Along the way
I saw you born a gift from heaven
A lifetime of love forever
From the first sound you made
To the first word you spoke
Happiness is the gift you gave
And joy is what I felt
For the future I cannot speak
But through you
Part of me may see
I am a dreamer
What I hope can come true
When I was young I lived free
That is what I wish
For you to be...

Punky

It's coming down beside me
And soaking in my bones
I want to scream for help
Because I feel so alone

Can you know the feeling
Or the hurt
Of leaving a good friend
Lying in the dirt?

I open my eyes
Can't let them blink
Weakness in my knees
My blood begins to freeze

The night will decide
In that moment
I can only wait
Everything I know forgotten

It's coming down beside me
And soaking in my bones
I want to scream for help
Because I feel so alone

Muscles move my mouth
Words won't come out
I try to shout!

Just wanted you to know
Something you'll never read

A letter to myself
To say goodbye to you

The words drop
From my throat
Onto the paper

I was saved by a hair
The right time
The right place
Can't make you go

Wish you to be somewhere else
Wished I'd never asked
Did you come because of fate?

I stood and shivered
At your last bubbles of breath
Life from your body
Gone like vapor

It's coming down beside me
And soaking in my bones
Like water washed from a stone
All that's left are tears
For my friend

Walk with me one more time
You're still young and I am old
You're still my friend

Your memory
I will always hold

Blacksmith's Hammer

A long thin bead
And a blacksmith's hammer
A horseshoe hangs
Above the door

An empire surrounds the emperor
He has nowhere to stand
As it expands

Fossils lay handcuffed
Under the ground
Yes, as you gaze and dig
You will find things that astound
I have been
By some of the things
I've found

Follow the fluid
As it flows out
An empire and emperor
That's what it's about

High compression cylinder bore
It moves like a cyclone
The sound is violent
But I love the roar

Eye and tooth are what
We're looking for
We'll find it with a little luck
From above the door

Find the key, open the lock
The next step you take
Will seal your fate
Speed is a must
No time to decide
There's no telling where
What you're looking for will hide

Once uncovered, you must act...
Then sail on the wind...
Floating forever with time...

You Laugh Back

Just like watching water flow
It smiled at me
I laughed back
Locked in earth's cradle
No windows to see

Cobwebs hang
 Like long, thin wire
They burn real fast
When set on fire

When plenty
They seem like fog
And sometimes it reeks
Like an old dead log

Spiders walk so fast
But they look slow
 Just like watching
Water flow

It smiled at me, I laughed back
Then it crawled away
From where did it come?
Where does it go?

Millions are born, then grow
Just like watching water flow
A place to hide, never to be found
Where the weathers warm
All year round

Caught...
In the web of life
Hanging from a long, thin wire

Fog and dust, eternity of fire
They survive alone
Never in a pack

If they smile at you
Just laugh back

Waiting

Every day I wait for spring
It's in no hurry to arrive
Teasing me with gentle sunshine
And warm breezes
Ice thaw
Streams down the mountain side
First a drip
Flows wrap the stones
Polishing them
Before being dried
By the sun
The air is crisp
With the smell of new life
Blowing through the trees
Old leaves crackle and break
Under my feet as I walk
Here I sit under a pine
Next to the river
Chunks of ice melt as they pass
A meeting place unknown to all
Slowly the sun floats up
It blends into the morning sky

Birds chirp and bugs crawl
Butterflies dance around my head
I sit and wait
Wishing to be in another place
Slowly I blink as I brush a bee
From my brow
Hours and hours have gone
But still I remain
Now the sun falls to the horizon
And hides behind a hill
A chill in the air
Shiver in my bones
Soon I want to go
Darkness covers the sky
Stars twinkle in my eye
Waiting is hard work
As far as I can tell
Forbearance is not in my blood
Waiting and sleeping
Are much alike
So until tomorrow
I wish you goodnight

Just for an Instant

Sitting under a tree
That's growing in the yard

Writing a letter
My heart's beating hard

Traveling across the land
Touching you with my hand

I see you walking
My way

My mind scrambles
For something to say

Down the slippery slide
you come

I wait at the bottom
With a song I hum

Children climb up the tree
Down the stairs the people flee

On the clouds I float
Watching waves from a boat

Catching a fish from a pond
With new friends I bond

Playful in the afternoon
Roasting marshmallows
By the moon

Hide and seek is the game
In my memory are the names

Some grow old, others not
Like thunder horses trot

In their echo is the cry
Fight for freedom or we die

Life and love both grow
The seeds we eat
And seeds we sow

The wind on my lips as I sleep
A kiss, a tear, a mountain steep

Disappointment grips
And it holds tight
The prize you seek is in sight

To wish and hope
The end of the rope

Under the tree in the yard
Branches bend, but still hard

This is where I am
Among the wolves, a lamb

The leaves fall to the ground
Silent without a sound

There they stay and wait
On a hook, the bait

Double track, two trains meet
With loads of ore and wheat
Under the bridge
The sky moves fast

The flag flies high
Above the mast
On the rocks the waves strike
Tiring from the weary hike

Frozen in ice
A tumble of the dice
Victory at hand
The fight over ownership of land

In the end
The wind will blow
Then it decides
Where the leaves will go

Buried in the ground
Never to be found

Bricks, trees, bones
Pieces of stones

Writings
Pictures of the past
This knowledge is vast

In my life, I should learn
Stand in line and wait my turn

Patience I have, but cut short
King and Queen
Joker of the court

Clothes and style
Everyone's on trial

Tribes of color and tradition
We put our names on petitions

Come over to our side
This is a good place to hide

In an instant
A picture is made
To sell, buy, and trade

I wait for an answer
To the letter I sent

Watching the branches
Of the tree going bent

In time, my body does the same
To the question, is life a game?

No, it's a journey
It's a trip
For the weak and for the fit

Time, space, star and light
Wrong and right

This is what we all know
Birth, then life, we grow

A circle, a shape
Fix it with tape

Time is early and it's late
Love and hate
Laws we pass
Green is the color of the grass

Below my feet, there is no doubt
Into the big blue sky I shout
Here I am
Please see me
Under the shade of the tree

With tears I cry
Upon joy I sing

Throughout the land
Bells will ring

For the journey is not done
Until the game is won
So do not give up or quit
Leave the candle lit
This glow of light
Wind that fills a kite

Your destination is in your heart
Love and devotion
Is how you start
Day after day, never end
Expectation is around the bend

Now it's time to start the journey
Tomorrow I wake up early
Through the day without a worry
Take my time, never hurry
There is time for rest
But be ready for the test...

Inflexation

I hurt my fingers
As I hit the ground
People push and shove
To get out of town
There are no bounds
Where people will go
There is no limit to their control

Childhood is where
We have all stood
We challenge the leader
Thinking we'll win
Watch the calendar
And the clock
Sit frozen in shock

Since the time we could crawl
Colored drawings
Disguise the wall
You must obey, it's the law
Do nothing, but watch the wall

Stand in the center of the round
Where lies and truths are found
Dirt and dust float in the air
It sticks to your hair

Walk until you find the gate
Inside you find people
Who love and hate
Time in my pocket, but a blur
Who can you trust?
You're not sure

Point your finger
In any direction
Doors explode into dust
With this roar, winds gust
You're not weak
You are strong
Think it...
Show it...
Live it...

Station

A girl walks past
She laughs at me
Looks like a tattoo
On a broken-hearted soul

Gives me directions
Tells me where to go

Telephone rings
No one answers the call
Lots of numbers on the wall

Wonder how long
This place stays open
Will they ever lock the door?
People talk, it echoes a roar

A whistle, a buzzer, a bell
Always something new
My eyes are feeling heavy
Hum a morning tune

Some people speak funny
In the morning air
As if they were never there

Plaid shorts and a yellow shirt
How much can they be worth?

A vacation land for women
Children and men
Ribbons that never end

Follow the signs
Arrows painted
Lockers, lounge and baggage

Restrooms, tickets, taxis
Lost and found
A blue telephone

This is a big place
I feel alone
Sixteen windows
All of them closed

Keys hanging on a belt
Mops hit the floor

Big, old pipe
Newspaper under his arm

He's walking fast
It's getting warm

Falling asleep
One second more

Twenty-four hours
I woke up on the floor

My bag's getting heavy
Is this what I really need?

Still looking for
Home sweet home

?...

Forever

Moving in every direction
On the left and right
They are all around
In front and behind

Where are they going?
All in a line

It's dark, this hole in the ground
We have freedom
Nowhere to go
The yard has become too small
A place to camp is all

Sometimes
I long for the time
Of my past and my youth

Playing in a tree
Running up a hill
Endless, endless time to kill

Now I count every minute
I see it everywhere
It's on my arm
Carried in my mind
Another place
Is where I want to be

Be ...
Someone once said
Is studied by men
Who are told they're great
I am what I am
Until I die in my bed
What comes after time ceases?
Great men, please tell me

Some read from paper
A few from crystal balls
Some ask themselves

Before the answer
There must be a question
That is where the answer must be

It's just a mark
At the end of a sentence
The end is a good place to start

So it's not the answer we seek
And the question we know

Is it time itself
That holds the key?
What is the question
If time is the answer?

Something that time
And everything has
A beginning and an end you say

I think it's forever
Because time will never end
To be has already happened

Not to be is the end...

Memories in Ink

The gifts given to me
I sometimes take for granted
They cannot be bought
Or wrapped in ribbons or bows
So much I have received
 It has become expected
Like the rain and sun
Or the air that I breathe
Where do they come from?
 Who gives them to me?
Why do I want more?
 My needs are slight
The memories I keep
 Have more value
The things I tell my children
Are linked to me forever
An unbroken chain of thoughts
From my memory
To be shared with others
At some unknown time

A rainbow of memories reach
A place that none can ever go
Only hear about and only know
Somewhere is a place
And that is where I am
Somewhere can be a memory
Or a place in time
Somewhere can never be lost
But it can be found
A place to go
Around and around
A special sound
Echoes through the sky
Through the ground
Through my body and mind
Reflections of my life
Others and everything I see
The endless river will never end
It will flow on to another
Through word and pen

It grows
As a garden
Of
Memories...
Ideas ...
Loves ...
Desires...
Hopes, and wishes...
The garden of an endless cycle
In a limited life
The words and deeds live on
Without water or sunlight
They are left in the soil
To be found someday
A country, a state
A future supplied with a past
Left only to fate
Passed on to others
Through an invisible link...
Of memories and ink...

Singing

Birds sing in the morning
Without a thought
How can they do so
Without being taught?

I work in the concrete jungle
Mundane life of sweat and toil
This is where buildings reach the sky
Made by men of design
From a different history and time
Everything at my fingertips
Any desire
People make this place
They wear rags
Some wear lace

Some work hard, others beg
A few demand
Here's to the birds
Looking for a home
Without forest or trees

Between a sea
Of concrete buildings
Are the gems of green
Where the birds play and sing

I go there and close my eyes
I go where happiness cries
They sing like innocent children

Flowers of spring
Everything fresh and new
Washed by drops
From the river of life
A waterfall from the sky
Soaked up by all
Creatures kind and gentle
Or guilty of sin

Trustworthy and loyal
A song not everyone sings
Even the birds
Have clans and tribes
They protect home and land

We all signal each other
Signs of peace
Wave a hand, blink an eye
Some agreements hold
 Most won't I'm told
Unless it's signed in blood

Sing with joy when at the top
Or when sad, never stop
Songs from the heart can heal
A song from the heart is real
Sing like a bird
An ascending circle of sound
Pierces the air
A sweet melody
Dances through your head

For innocent children
And flowers of spring
It is a great design

Let the sound ring!

Heartbeat

Rhythm, how does it work?
It's in life
Sound, wood, stone
And the food we eat
The oceans are filled
With waves that beat

The wind tears the waves
Rips the water
Part of it falls, then breaks free
It's powerful like chains of iron
Dragging away an anchor
I follow the pulse
My own heartbeat out of control

Peace is reached by some
They try to show us the way to go
It's their path
I cannot follow sound
Not meant for me
My heartbeat is the bell I hear
I follow my compass

Not by some chance
Or without direction
When I see the light shine
My heart tells me to follow

Light has a rhythm and a shape
A chain of love out of the earth
With a golden glow
We sing to it
Like a king on a throne
A piece of golden stone

It shares my life
Protects me from the storm
How can this be so?
A piece of metal keeps me safe
Something I wear around my neck
Will help me win a race

The heartbeat, the soul
I live with it on my face

I asked for the unknown
Be shown to me
My eyes to be opened
The door to be torn down

The power and glory frightens me
A wish that cannot come true
Until life is given in whole?
One foot on the land
The other in the sea

You must bend your knee
Wish for a rainbow
Clouds to be free
Go beyond branches
Reach the sky
Touch waves

Flow with the wind
Live on the air
Breathing in life forever

Birth

She was lying on the bed
Waiting for the time
My thoughts were of wonder
I could see and feel the moment
They were moving a lot
Especially at night
Could they hear the world
They were coming into?
She waited night after night
A few weeks until the date
Would they come early or be late
The sun smiled, the moon beamed
On another October day
Tonight could be the night
For two new lives
To shine like stars
Glowing with love on energy
From high above

Early in the morning
But still dark, cool, and quiet
Silence of the night
Echoed in the air
She awoke for it was time
Then it happened
Sight of life, birth of babies
Into the world they came
With their little legs
From a secret hiding place
Into the world of stars
They grow slowly, then soar
Standing on their toes
Reaching for wonder
Hearts full of joy
Destiny will pass with youth
Love and truth
Words of language, sense of feeling
Off they go, on their way
A beautiful song
Left in my memory

Thoughts

Here no one knows my name
They listen and wonder
Why and how

Applause and cheer
In this they give me what I seek
But this may be a lie

All alone in the cold
Air biting a stone
Running to a different time
Looking for old friends

A wish for the road
No armor, gun or gold
Only my hand, I offer to hold

Darkness falling over my eyes
I wait for tomorrow's sun
For life's magic is fun
Walking on the side of the road

Someone to love and to hold
Lying on the side of the road
A hot day, but night gets cold

Wind and river flow
No one knows why
Years go by like grains of sand

Church bells ring
A strong sound floats to my ear
Forests and trees crowds of people
Wrongs are forgiven

Bare feet walk on grass
Tickle a smile
Throw away the meaningless noise

Life's energy moves
Let your lips touch
Then embrace
In this instant you will love

The Leader

A place to sit, a place to play
A place to spend the day
Running fast, jumping high
Spinning round and round

Climb to the top
Slide to the ground
Find a new friend
Play with them
Again and again

Sit under a tree
Branches of shade
Looking at the hills
That the ants have made
Bicycles parked here and there
Some on the ground without a care

Carve my name into a tree
My friend and I
For everyone to see

A water fountain stands nearby
We drink and splash
A big basket that holds trash

Up the tree the children go
A new adventure to live and know
Be the leader or one of many

Watch and you can learn
Follow today's command
Energy, speed, and strength
Youth has an endless supply

Everyone wants to climb
The mountain high
Push and shove to get ahead
Some fall and try again

One more time or stay at the bottom
Another day will come
Time is young
Like the fire burning sun

The walk home
Brings memories of the day
Suddenly I say
I'm tired and hungry
Home I go

The welcome is a pleasant tone
It wraps around me
Like a blanket of love
Into my bed I go to dream
My eyes close to the day
My dreams come to life

It's nothing like I've ever seen
At the bottom of the hill
Stand my forces
March up the hill
Then charge
Full speed
The course is straight
The fastest we've ever run

No one falls
To the top we go
Birds float
Above in the sky
A finger tip away

Water running
Between the rocks
A small cave I see
To my troops I say
Be heroes and follow me

If anyone gets lost
Meet at the big oak tree
With roots like steps
And names carved in time
For everyone to see...

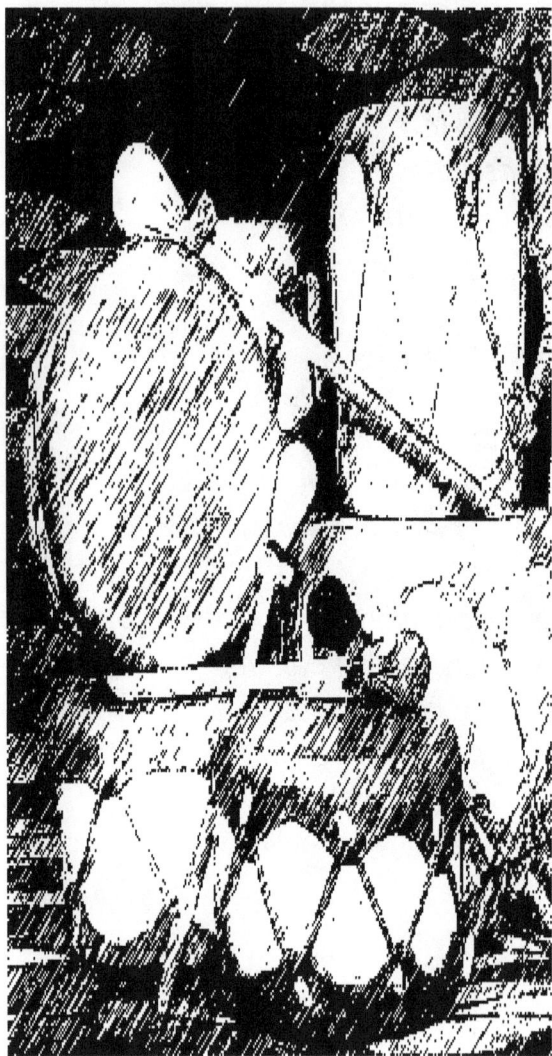

Drumbeat

Can you hear it vibrate
Through the trees
Around our bodies
And into the mountains
Humming bee's sting
As the sound hits the breeze
I count, my foot moves
Along with the sound
An invisible connection
Known to everyone
Language is spoken sound
A Heartbeat pounds
Rolling like a wheel
Down the highway
Against the hull of a ship
In the bay waiting
For the captain to sail away
Up comes the wind
Waves pound each other
Between the ships
In the bay they are pinned

Out moves a ship
High on a wave
Out toward the sun
To follow the drumbeat
Until the day is done
A new foreign place
In nature where law is design
Made at the moment and time
Decisions are carried out
It accepts no interruption
To the cadence
Black and white
Just a little gray
Some rhythm with melody
Bells toll and ring free
Sending vibration
Through space and time
Waiting to be heard
A gift and a treat
That is what some call
The drumbeat

By man, bird or beast
There is a sound
From the earth
Movement under the ground
Silence comes
We shudder and shake
We stop in our tracks
The next step afraid to take
Where's the drumbeat
My foot tries to find the step
Mountains crush and grind
Upward to the sky
Slowly they go
They seem not to move
Slowly streams of water
Take it away
My foot looks for the sound
It moves on the ground
The drumbeat will guide you
Just follow the sound

Mirror

Glass and sand
A most delicate surface
Hard and smooth
See through and reflect

From the time
When I was young
To now when I'm old
Everything has changed

I've sold and bought
Borrowed and begged
I've given and taken
But still not forsaken
Guided by a dream or was it real?

So long ago
But in my mind still fresh
The promise will be kept
As told to me

As I climb
Stepping from branch to branch
Running from the truth
That scared me so

They said I didn't know
Not only did I know
But cried when told

When asked
How do you know?
Tears ran down my face
Their pain I felt burn my soul

Then I felt a gentle hand
Soothed my head
This gentle touch never felt

Down I climbed
And ran home fast
All were there
And more tears flowed

Now it's the promise I fear
For the time is near
The stage is set and all will cheer
This moment waits for me
As my hair turns gray
And my bones grow thin

This dance please, I must ask?
To no longer see
The reflection in glass
That person is gone
Never to return

The mirror doesn't lie
No more time can be bought
No amount of money
Can be paid

The cost of nothing
The price for something
Every day this I see
When I wake and look

I see my memories and promises
When I wake and look
Touch the glass, it's the same
But I have changed
How can this be?

A reflection that grows old
Someday when I look
I will see the answer
That has taken so long

I will touch the mirror
Feel where time has gone
And taken me

I will not know
Who it is I see
I will be back up in the tree

The gentle touch
Will always set me free!

Job

Do you hear the ringing?
It's warm under the covers
Safe in my nest
Curled up like a baby
Waiting for soft fingers
To caress me
The dream is over now
I must wake
Still I hear the ringing
Again and again
Eyes open, muscles stretch
And my bones crack
Slowly I stand
To get my balance
Two feet planted
Firmly on the floor
I make my way over to the door
Down the stairs
One step at a time
The rail guides me down
In a straight line

Splash water on my face
Comb and brush
Spray the plants
So they look lush
Coffee aroma floats into my nose
My hatred for this job grows
Shoes are on, the door is shut
Off to the bus
The groove has become a rut
There must be something better
Coming my way
Skies are not always gray
Train ride after train ride
Is this my home?
So many hours
A good place to write a poem
Where are the fields of grain
And the forest green?
Put my clothes
In the washing machine
Hang them on the line
Go to the store
Shop for some more

What to wear, I don't know
Matching from here to there
Head to toe
What color socks and shoes
Make a decision, win or lose
Time to choose
A little space please
Celebration is my choice
A chance to raise my voice
Plan for this and plan for that
Do a little or do a lot
Choose to or choose not
Give or take, real or fake
Work for yourself
Or for someone else
Why work at all? Try to be free
Just live and have a ball
Open your eyes
See time pass quickly
Never will it come again
Every moment a jewel
Value beyond belief
Stolen by time, the thief

Slight of hand, the world today
Now you see, now you pay
Nothing in return
Except lessons to learn
If you're lucky
A chance for success
To win the top prize
Excitement bubbles in your eyes
Tell everyone you know
With a smile
This is the way it should be
Everyone's a winner
Before they get old
In my mind it begins
A wish, then hope
Will change come my way?
Locked in a box without a key
Only a window to watch and see
How can I break free?
The answer so simple
Can you see?

Open the door, stand at the edge
Knees shake, I might fall
Gravity a true law
Learn how to fall
Land on your feet
Not on your back
No net to soften the blow
Perfection and luck
This is your time
It's now passing by
Your choice
Sit, stand or jump
Not knowing how you'll land
The moment is here
Choose you must!
It's for you to decide
To start and stop the ride
Your eyebrow will rise
Lick your lips
Touch your chin
Make the choice to win!

White Clouds in Blue

Watch while fingers
Move up and down
Sound echoes in my head
This is what I want to create
Sound so beautiful, wind on a lake
Gentle, rough, and mean wind
Power beyond human touch
Notes, many and few
High on a wing
Out from waves they flew
Twinkle at night
White clouds in blue
Taste of an apple sweet on my lips
Punishment with whips
Callous and hard they become
You fall in love with the pain
Sound all around, falling rain
Into fire and water below
Apart and together
Onward you flow

Sounds bend and peak
Notes are strong and weak
Almost silent to the listener's ear
Others bold enough to tear
Power that cannot be explained
Deep to the touch to release the fear
Once you light the candles wick
Fire will burn and melt away
Barriers that block you
From the light
In the presence of greatness
Bright star to bright star
From where did the sound come?
Shooting across the sky
Down to the ocean deep
Heavy waves that crack as thunder
Lightning and a sting
Then over just as quick
A blink of an eye
Gone forever never to return
The music left for others to learn

Age & Glory

Have you heard the big bang?
It's growing older day by day
We age and turn gray
Do the stars disappear?
Do they burn away?
What do they pass?
What do they give?
A light to follow
And show the way
What takes their place?
How are stars born anyway?
Like balls of light
High above in the night
Powerful, no limit to their might
People talk about shapes
They see in the sky
Some kind of animal
Or bird that flies

Pictures of them are everywhere
Faces on planets
Everyone searches for the rock
That holds the secrets
Of the cosmic clock
Stones in circles
Space in between
Unless you can fly
They can't be seen
Every angle is precise as can be
Geometric shapes
At the bottom of my tea
A lot of confusion
No one can agree
Looking for a link
From the ice frozen ground
Layer upon layer
Nothing is found
Continue the search
Look for the answer
To the beginning
Can this be the way?

Bone, stone, finger, or tooth
Look for the star
Where the light never dims
This is the way to see forever
Not the night
Always the light looks new
Stand together, it takes two
Deception, lies, pain and joy
Honest and true blue
Believe only what you see
Just a small part of life
Union of light
The age is bright
Escape the body and skin
Wait for the light
To signal...
Then begin...
Just the first step is a challenge
That can stop or break
It may take a lifetime to climb
Seem impossible to make

One possible solution is clear
Wash away and kill the fear
It's a trap for young and old
Age will come, of that no doubt
How do we stop age?
The people shout!
What can I purchase
To stay young?
This is what many
Have dreamed
Carved in marble
The stone stands alone
Weather away slowly
In front of our eyes
Suffer in battle
Screams and cries
Soldiers are first
To understand
Battle and war
Must be won
Live forever
Through your son

The moment of truth
Why me at this time?
Will someone write
About my life?
Will anyone read?
Win the battle
To go beyond
Tell your children
Before they dream
A bedtime story
Night will come, then go
You will age
You think slow
Time will change
This is for sure

A question you must answer
Is this the time for glory?

Behind the Thumb

With one eye closed
I glance at my thumb
Behind it a face or tree
Bird or place
Perhaps a waterfall or rainbow
Lightning from the sky
An insect crawling up the wall
A mouse smiling
At a piece of cheese
Maybe a raindrop melting
Into the pavement
Anything I please
Behind the thumb, a secret place
All my very own, very small to see
But endless and precious to me
No canvas or paint or special light
No brush to shape
The image from sight
With one eye closed
And one thumb high

A girl who needs to cry
Trains that go by
Boys fighting on a step
A small child chasing a dog
Her mother calls
Faces peering out bus windows
With an intense stare
Space is getting more and more rare
Airplanes overhead
Ships sailing past
Buildings reaching up
Touching the sky
Some mountains I see
Musical notes
Instruments of sound
A choir sings
Men and women dance
My childhood friends
Games we played
My pet dog digging for a bone
The baby pig
My Dad brought home

Christmas and birthdays and gifts
Books I've read
My favorite hat
Blowing out of the car window
Things that have happened
Things that will be
This picture I paint
With one eye closed
And one thumb high
Sadness and joy
Round tables, square bricks
Piles of trash
Paid for with piles of cash
Long skirts, mini-skirts
Neckties and socks
Diamonds are my favorite rocks
Waterfalls of silver
Pour into pools of water
No logos, cans, bridges or stores
There was a time long ago
Or so it seems to me
Before movies and television
Newspaper print

Spaceships, schools and apple pie
All people had was a precious place
In their minds eye
With one eye closed
And one thumb high
Now small tables, chairs, pencils
Crayons everywhere
Paper, pictures, colors of rainbows
In the sky it glows
Hills in the distance
Under the clouds
Flowers growing everywhere
Glimmering streams
Dance over stones
A smell of wheat in the air
Eating watermelon under a tree
Exploring the woods with my dog
Playing with and catching frogs
Collecting shiny rocks
All my memories flash by
With one eye closed
And one thumb high

Champions of Glory

Truth without lie
Solid color, ask why
Rain or wind in my face
Better not lose an important race
Gold medals and trophies
Ribbons of silk
Pictures of smiles
Charge fast to the base
Home run over the fence
Flash the checkered flag
Hole in one, take the bait
Up the middle touchdown
Down the hill fast
Sell or buy
Nothing ever lasts
Luck of the draw, not every time
Getting old, no longer in my prime
Take a chance
Do your best
Believe you can
Don't worry about the rest

We've read of this
In myth and story
Trumpets roar, crowds cheer
For champions of glory
Fierce warriors they are
Abundance of courage
Never tasting fear
Look the opponent in the eye
Make them give in
Not even try
Filled with strength
More energy than you know
Thunder and lightning
Strike with a trust
But someday
Green wood bends
Old wood withers
Then crumbles to dust
Just as champions of glory
Someday must

War on Nature

Alaska oil pipeline
Ringing in the wilderness
Digging never stops
Acid rain, melting trees
Around the mountain lakes
River polluted fountains
Air thick as morning fog
Forests filled with vertical logs
Ferocious attack
Everything's turning black
Laws to make us be good
Enjoy the wild forever
Prosperity the killer
Carmakers, real estate
Oil tycoons
Logging and mining
Will business stop
The stars from shining?
Decade after decade
Laws are made

Promotion of the environment
Nature will fade
Life as we know it, a grim future
A fairy tale or true
Which side to fight
Many have no clue
Criminal action, fines to pay
Deep pockets, time to make hay
Dark ages return from the past
The plague is back
Walk or be carried away
Earth day, species of many kinds
Celebration for all
Right wing, left wing, tail feather
Shadow of a blue print
Let's build it today
Apocalypse, heresy, lies
From both sides
Lawyer counsel, what's the plan?
Enforce the law
Pay what you can
I'll win the case if not start again

Public revolt in the world
Free speech for all
Pay for your sin, no way to win
Exploit the system
Attack the tribe
Pedal your goods
Sell your wares
Sweetheart deals
To make gold rich men
The agenda is cheating
Stealing to hoodwink
An optimistic view
Water and sky are blue
The colors will change
Is what some say
How can it be?
Help us, help us
Please grow a tree
Where there are none to see
Garbage, plastic, metal, glass
Where can I buy some gas? ·

The greatest invention known
Wheel or the can
Stagnate life, ruler of men
Recycle or use less
One hundred years from now
I can't guess
In my youth
I climbed trees to the top
Now there's a mess
Grab a bucket and mop
Modern pollution
An endless amount
Earth day once a year
Time for everyone to shout
This is also a business
For a few jobs
Your vote will change laws
Rebel for our national treasures
For old and gray
Be part of the government
Maybe that's the way

A rich man's club
A senior career
Cloaked in secrecy
And hidden agenda
Our pyramid eye sees all
Pass the buck to the office
Down the hall
Election money
Give me your vote
I'll make your life
Sweet musical notes
Promise to do nothing
Complain about everything
Energy we need more
Will dig right through
The ocean floor
Buy a big house
And fill it with more
Freedom we fight
For what's left
While wise men speak
And make deals
Who do I want to be?

Right or wrong,
Guilty or innocent
Swim fast through life
We'll all meet in the end
Leaving our memories
For others to tend
Battles and wars
Again and again
Just a soldier
Going where I'm told
Thinking why
And when will it change
Dream every day
Hope for tomorrow
Turn like the earth
Night and day
Light from the moon
Tide from the bay
Be noble and brave

Pushing Buttons

Everywhere I look
Dumb kids doing dumb things
I saw it with my children
Pushing elevator buttons
Fun, Fun, Fun
It comes easy for them
Cardboard boxes can be anything
A car, a house, a ship, or a cave
What I think may be dumb
Is it a smart way to behave?
Once you leave this world of play
It's often impossible to return
Try and try as you may
Again and again
Our knee-high world
Begins to grow
Play world shrinks
Fun stops to flow
Touched only at special moments
Rare times in your life

Banging on pots and pans
No fun anymore
Color and paint
For your imagination too hard
Now aware and always on guard
Careful and suspicious
Of all that's around
Looking for the playtime world
It may be lost forever
Again, never found
Growing up day by day
Every minute counted
It shapes life like a piece of clay
Running free with a dog
Rolling on the ground as we play
Riding in the back
Of a pickup truck
Wind in our faces
Playing ball, hitting home runs
Going around the bases
I still hear kids cheer
That moment is very old indeed

Grandma and Grandpa
In the garden with smiles
Flowers bloom from a tiny seed
Falling on the gravel
Tearing my knee
This pain is the same
And will always be
Learning how to wiggle my ears
Finding fossils
Digging in a cave
Tunnels that connect
In some far away land
Walking in a stream without a care
Catching frogs
Collecting them in pails
Hundreds of butterflies
Floating through the trees
Horses eating grass
Football season catching a pass
One off the fingertips
It falls to the ground
Gasps roar about the air

Friends good and bad
Unknown to them
Simple life and fun
Telephone jokes
Card games, losing bets made
Life is hard and sometimes cruel
Accident and broken bones
A close friends dies
Broken promises and lies
Which path, the way is not clear
Play at high speed
Not just for fun, but greed
Trying for success
I think this is what I need
Failure always at my heels
Playtime is short, no time for fun
Now too old to run
Internet, online, e-mail my friends
Tools and toys
Playtime for girls and boys

Riding the elevator
With my kids
Race in and race out
Whose fingertips touch first?
Let out a shout
The cardboard box is mine
Excitement explodes
For them fun comes easy
Everywhere they look
Feel sad if you fall
Push some buttons on the wall
There's wonder left
For everyone to see
Fun above and beyond
For dumb kids like me
And for people too old to run
Can't go back to play
I say never leave
Hands of time shape the clay

A Basket of Flowers

A world full of flowers
Carried by my friend
Weaved together
So beautiful to see

Looking for a place to rest
Next to a stream
On a hill or under a tree
Soft grass between my toes
Brushing tall flowers
With my fingertips

Tilt my head upward to the sky
Warm sunshine falls
On my face
This is all free
There's nothing to buy
This could be
The perfect place

I hear and see water splashing
Over the rocks
It reminds me of a bride
With a veil over her face

Steps of stones
Go up along the hill
Stopping for a moment
Standing still, clouds float past
Flags of the world, high on a mast

Bees and butterflies
Fly between the trees
My heart pounds with every breath
A lone plum tree in my path
With beads of glistening juice
Falling to the grass

Rolling down the hill
Laughing drunk
From the spring water
Bubbling out of the ground

The scent of hot air
Tickles my nose
Crystal leaves
Flicker and shake
While they drop to the ground

Fields of flowers
A bright colored rainbow on a hill
Only one basket I have to fill

Into the basket
The flowers go
For a gift, a present
Thanks and love
No strings attached
Give nothing in return

A basket of flowers
For love that burns
Like a rainbow from above

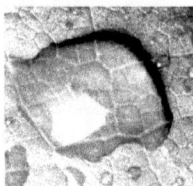

Jewelry Store Fly

This day is hot!
Heat from the sun and concrete
Penetrate into my body
The jewelry store catches my eye
Every jewelry store I pass
Catches my eye
You might say I'm
A jewelry store fly
Up to the window I go
Looking at everything that glows
Long, long, long, long, long, long
Everything shines and shimmers
I see diamonds and gold
Rings and watches
Hands go round and round
Time ticking away
Number by number, count the days
Long, long, long, long, long, long
It all shines and shimmers
Glass in the display
Ice on a hot day

Black stones, green rocks,
Red gems
Gold and silver chains
Money down the drain
Looking for treasure
This is what I do
Traveling from shop to shop
A farmer checking the crop
This is all mine to view
Step by step, window by window
In displays appear
Jewelry you can wear
On your hands and feet
Through your nose or ear
Around the neck
Chain links of gold, tons are sold
New design under my feet
It stood for my eye alone
Color and tone, twinkling shone
A circle in the middle of a square
Gray all around the wall
Rising up from the ground
Under my shoe it went

My eye scanning people
A beam of light that's bent
Rainbows of color
Spawn reflections that dent
Ripples of water
The edge of the shore
Keyhole and a seam of light
Catches dust from under the door
Hanging in the air
A floating candle flare
Burning so bright
Long, long, long, long, long, long
I've waited to find this jewel
And there it was
Right under my shoe
Hands over my face
Breathing room at last
Tomorrow I search again
For a new prize never seen
More real than I know
A wish, hope
And a new dream

Come Inside

Come inside to me
I'll give you a place to hide
Come inside to me
I'll protect you is what I cried
By the hand hold on tight
Follow me through the night
Careful, don't slip or fall
Listen to the wind call
One more word to you
Then silent we become
Run fast at my side
Never let go of the bond
Your soft touch
Forever and beyond
Nothing ever I've loved so much
An embrace we are free
Open sky above
A blanket of stars open and wide
Come inside to me
I'll protect you is what I cried

Broken and Bent

Up to the sky I looked
Blue, white, and diamonds at night
Over there, a tree I saw
Another world in a nest
Babies standing on the edge
The challenge, the test
This barrier had no limit
They were not gravity bound
An impulse to be free
In the begining only seconds
Just a few feet
Back to safety to rest
Next, high aloft, gazing below
In command wherever they fly
Miraculous I thought
And I tried to imagine
What it was they saw
Down I looked
To the wagon I pulled
Bright red, black and white wheels

If only I had wings
I'd know what a bird feels
Night after night I dreamed
What binds me to the ground
In my dreams I could fly
There was no law
So wings of cardboard and wood
I made for my wagon with wheels
To the top of the hill I climbed
As the sun set in the west
Break free of the barrier
That ties me down
Into my wagon
My heart began to pound
With great speed
I traveled to the edge
Then let out a cry
Waiting for the wind
To take me up to the sky
Seconds felt like hours
And a whole day
In this time I could imagine
What birds could view

Liberated from gravity
My dreams came alive as I flew
The barrier, gravity and limit
The challenge I met
Broken wings, bent wagon
A short celebration
Back home to my nest
A milestone I've taken
The stars are next
But one step at a time I thought
A few seconds and a few feet
The future is the sky
Beyond the diamonds of the night
The wagon is parked until this day
In my mind
Freedom, a bird on the wind
To see a glimpse
To live a moment of challenge
Again and again without a thought
Feel and live astonishment
Even though sometimes
All broken and bent

Three Lights on a Post

Cars are racing down the street
I hear footsteps on the pavement
Raindrops bouncing
Out of puddles of water
Reflections of street lights
Brilliant and bright
Wind blowing through the night
A girl I've never seen
Soaked to the bone
Standing under a tree
Then she looks at me
Lights on her face roll up into
The halo lit sky
Drops of rain let go of her hair
They pass down
Into the invisible ground
Like a ghost
Above her all aglow
Three lights on a post
There they shine
Sounds turn my head

Shadows echo from the silky street
My eye follows until they melt
Into the darkness
Now no one
Sits under the lamp post
Just an empty bench
Waiting for a passenger
To guide through the night
I taste mist in the air
Morning will come soon
Night disappears into the moon
Three lights pierce the night
The rain has stopped
And the mist is gone
A figure walks into my sight
Over to the bench
To rest for the night
Another passenger for this
Indiscriminate host
The new passenger gazes around
Content with what he has found
Sanctuary for a little while
Night watches from all around

No light from the post
Morning noise and blue skies
People laugh, babies cry
Dogs bark, bicycles squeak
An empty bench
Servant for the tired and weak
The day over and sun down low
The three lights begin to glow
And then a girl I've never seen
With lights on her face
Looks at me
Is she there on the bench
Or only a dream?
A reflection from the street
Passenger for the night
Waiting for someone
Three lights, one shadow
Place to wait for the day to come
I step down off the curb
Walk across the street
Into a world of reflection
Of day and night

To My Wife

Love is what I feel
Friendship
Is what we have
A hug, a kiss, a smile
When I think of you
Happy thoughts
Come my way!

www.slabypress.com

Books by John Siwicki

Poetry

Fences
The Poetry of Food and Drink
Warbles
Are You Casablanca

Novels

ExPRESSION

www.ingramcontent.com/pod-product-compliance
Lightning Source LLC
Chambersburg PA
CBHW061740020426
42331CB00006B/1308